The Great Highland

The Great Highland Adventure

Mark Hartley

ISBN: 9798329359916

The Great Highland Adventure

Copyright © 2024 Mark Hartley

All rights reserved.

No part of this book may be reproduced or used in any manner without the express written permission of the author.

Start

Hello, my name is David and I find school to be an interesting place with many different dynamics. The most interesting dynamic is the unwritten student hierarchy, with some people being deemed to deserve more respect and awe towards themselves than others. It is imaginary, but almost everyone in the year seems to be aware of it. The people that are perceived with the most stature recognise it from their peers and are usually the loudest in classrooms and around school. With that they carry a sense of entitlement, as a result. This was confirmed when someone told me that some people were pushing others around in the locker shed, and that it was 'the popular kids' at the bottom of it.

It also appeared that someone who seemed to be put in this category batted the most in softball, when we did it in PE. However, loyalty is very important to maximise your time in school, I find. Hence, I have Patrick, Noah and Jonathan to rely on for bonding at school. I have decided to write down a part of my school experience, with the inclusion of a school trip to the Highlands, and here it is.

Tuesday

Today was Tuesday and I looked at my timetable, which had Science as my first lesson of the day. This was a bit hit and miss, for enjoyment. This is because if we do an experiment it could be quite exciting. But today this particular person not once or twice but three times had their bag 'cabbaged' where all of their stuff was taken out of their bag, their bag then turned inside out, with everything put back in after before it being zipped back closed. After was English, but this time I was the victim of this act. It was nearing the end of the year, so some people's focus was low. Hence, there was this act of mischief in our class to do this to me, but only once thankfully. In days that had gone by I had built up a stock of orange juice cartoons in my bag, and after I had got it back I noticed someone drinking an orange juice cartoon, which made sense when I started to undo the treachery that had been incurred on my bag. This is because of course; there were no orange juice cartons left inside my bag. The cheek!

Loyalty

At least there was a little bit of respite at break time because I could rely on Patrick, Noah and Jonathan for some distancy. Then someone asked if any of us were willing go to the canteen with them. In response Noah asked "what for?" I suspect that people around school are a bit frightened of being seen by themselves, so they would rather have someone for companionship and moral support, but also to prevent the risk of them being laughed at for being by themselves and told that they have no friends. Sometimes people can be very cruel, sadly.

Art

Next was Art, which was the sort of lesson by this time of the year that we knew what work we had to do. So we did it at quite a relaxed pace, with some conversation. A lot depended on who you were sitting with because sometimes it felt that you weren't being included in the conversation on the table, thus making the experience less pleasant. On this occasion, I was with two other great lads, and it was actually quite enjoyable. During the lesson I required a glue stick and I saw one on another table so I thought I'd collect it.

But all of a sudden two people, who are put near the top of the imaginary hierarchy, came straight at me. I didn't give in though and held my ground. As a result, they went back to their table after they realised that I wouldn't succumb to intimidation. Furthermore, it's shameful when people suck up to others in the classroom. One of the two people told me to be quiet, and then someone else said "yeah David", so I told them to not be a suck up. I couldn't just stand by and not respond to this activity of wanting to climb the social hierarchy, by this chap. I place myself inside of the circle. Not on the outside, trying to reach the top, but inside away from it all. Although, it seems that if you don't just allow certain people in the classroom to walk over you, they notice and target you. I'd still rather that option though, instead of allowing people to walk over me.

Drama

Next was Drama, which gave our class a sigh of relief. This is because there's less pressure, during the lesson. It was performance day in Drama where we were expected to put on a performance to demonstrate what we'd learned over the past term. Our group wasn't exactly the most gifted in drama but we wanted to give it a real go and try to pull something out of the bag. We preferred to do our performance near the end so we could build up excitement and be really up for it, when the time came. Our energy was greatly appreciated by the audience as we had a great time performing for the class and teacher's entertainment. By making our performance not serious and a joyful enterprise with twists and turns, it left the audience not knowing what was going to come next. As a result, they were left desperate and gasping for more along the way.

Lunchtime

Now it was lunchtime where there are sort of only really two options, play football on the astro or talk. So of course, I went for football and so did Noah, Patrick and Jonathan.

Football

Before we started on the astro the PE teacher told me that I had been selected for the football match this week. I decided I wouldn't play. There is a story behind my reason: the last time I was selected, the team played away at another school. I probably should've guessed I would be benched when I was picked. I suppose I thought, twelve players, what were the chances of me being the one sub. Furthermore, one chap couldn't play so there were going to be eleven players. But then some players thought they'd put someone else in the team to replace the missing player. Yes, you guessed it, I was the sub and played about fifteen minutes at the end. And even that wasn't the end of my ordeal before I got off the minibus that evening: I was abused verbally on the minibus for a lot of the way back to school.

Thus, I declined this time. I was only selected because I turned up to football at lunchtime regularly. However, my consistency in turning up was because I enjoy it, and it was also good exercise. I finally worked out to ignore the cloud of excitement and positivity and think rationally that I'd just be on the bench with a bunch of cruel people who I'm not friends with.

Another aspect of the whole experience of the away trip was that another player was giving me a barrage of abuse in the weeks leading up to the match, but when they were concerned they'd have to sit by themselves on the minibus they then, asked me if I'd sit next to them.

Geography

Then, there was Geography, where I witnessed one of the most unlikely moments of my school career. It was absolutely hysterical what entailed as a result of someone else's bag being 'cabbaged'. The victim of this crime broke the unwritten rule: they told the teacher on the person who had done it. This was actually quite refreshing for a change.

Wednesday

Science

The next day it was time to prepare for three science lessons in a row, and I bumped into Robert on the way to the first one, and we looked at each other, both knowing what we were in for. We did discuss the 'elephant in the room' about the brutality of what lay ahead but once we got into the classroom we got our heads down, readying ourselves to climb our mountain rather than just face it. To be fair to whoever organised the timetable, it was nice that the science lessons were one of each Biology, Physics and Chemistry because it gives us a bit of variety.

Biology had some energy to it, because the teacher wasn't static. An idea that I had recently enabled me to understand what the teacher was teaching us today quite nicely.

My idea

I found, in some lessons, it could be difficult at times being put on the spot in the classroom to a question I didn't know the answer to. It could be even more difficult sometimes because people may laugh at you, which could make it harder for me focus. So to deal with this I came up with the idea of using a revision guide. This is because it has the answers in it so I would have something to assist me with when I was put on the spot and just for general use to help me understand topics in the classroom. Somehow the whole class soon found out. I guess after I answered correctly what a genome was in a lesson once before was a clue that people had found out how I was able to answer questions without hesitation. There were major and quite loud hysterics from the class, on this occasion, especially after the teacher said that I was on fire that day.

At one point in Physics today, Mr Cambridge was wowed at some of the answers that I was plucking out of the air, and said that it was some serious knowledge. It meant a lot coming from him, I thought. I found it quite difficult to do practical tasks in front of the class and today I was asked by Mr Cambridge to close the blinds. Of course, the rest of the class was keen to watch me go about doing this. But I did struggle because I found I wasn't used to adjusting blinds because we have curtains at home, so I didn't really know how to operate them. So throughout my sequence of trying to successfully complete the objective, other class members found it quite comedic and laughed. Someone said that it happened to them when the teacher called them out by saying in a nice and jovial manner that when they yawn, they really go for it. After quite a successful physics lesson Mr Cambridge seemed to hear some murmurs, and asked me as I was walking out at the end of the lesson if I had used a revision guide. All I could do was tell the truth, so I did.

At break time today, we had a nice bit of one bounce action. For those of you asking 'why don't you play no bounce instead?' Well, that would be nice, but the ability of our group means we do need to be realistic. So by playing one bounce we were able to get some good rallies going that were actually quite satisfying until someone got a bit too much on their kick and the ball landed, and stayed, on the sports hall roof.

In Chemistry, Mr Latin had energy and would get involved with us in the lessons. So, although on paper it may not have actually sounded great, on classroom floors the science lessons were quite good today.

History

Then we were rewarded with a history lesson, which are quite nice because the teacher completely changed my experience of learning history at school. The year before I was in the corner and didn't find the lessons pleasant from being isolated. Whereas this teacher didn't implement a seating plan, so I was next to Patrick and Jonathan, and it was a much more enjoyable learning experience, as a result. Today's lesson was absolutely fantastic as because we just watched an hour of history videos. Every time a video finished, I thought are we going to have to do some writing now? But then another video would always be put on, until it was the end of the lesson. There was also the side emotion at the end of every video that would be 'please play the next one and don't say that's enough for today'.

Lunchtime

Lunchtime was the same again, hop into the changing room, deliver some encouragement and motivation, before we would head out and enjoy the football facilities. We had a good run around on the astro with some nice football being played, before we then headed to tutor group. Today was silent reading in tutor group, so we did that for fifteen minutes and then headed to the last lesson of the day.

Interesting lesson

The last lesson of the day was business studies and we were going through a new part of the topic. Thus, we were reading worksheets on it and learning new terms. One student was asked what a specific term was and they then went into a long description about random things, which was quite hysterical, but the teacher did call it pathetic. When we were supposed to discuss what we'd learned from the lesson in the last part around a big table, someone suggested that we should play the holiday game. We were a bit bemused as to what it was, as so was the teacher, hence it continued briefly. By the time everyone had started to understand the game, we realised how much of a nonsense it was. As the teacher could no longer be bothered with us, he said we could go. As we were walking out a student said "thanks mate" to the teacher. The teacher said in response "thanks for working so hard". This class was different to other classes because once to prevent having to do work one table talked to the teacher about food for about half an hour.

Thursday

Walk to School

Today we walked to school as usual, but Jonathan had forgotten to have breakfast. Not to worry though, he could just purchase something from the local supermarket. He went for a meal deal comprised of a smoked salmon and cream cheese sandwich, spicy orange crisps and a bottle of water. But the supermarket staff said that the school didn't allow students to be served before school. What a pity. So, Jonathan put his items back and while he was doing this Patrick suggested that he got a breakfast bap from the school canteen. "That'll do just fine", Jonathan said. Problem solved.

Then just as we walked into the canteen, the bell went and the staff started packing everything away. So, Jonathan said he would just have to go without food for a while. He then added "a bit of hardship in life is good".

First lesson

During our first lesson of today, there was a moment when the whole class was quiet and getting on with their work and Jonathan's stomach rumbled. Ah. Slightly awkward. But time is a great healer so everyone would soon forget about it, I thought. I had a similar scenario because I had spilt toothpaste on my blazer that morning, while I was brushing my teeth, and so there was a very noticeable white mark on the top part of my blazer.

IT

In second lesson, I was enjoying IT. It was great fun because there was an opportunity for a bit of creativity today. After that was break time, which was nice, although not a lot happening.

Maths

Maths was pretty uneventful today with it being simply a case of our heads being down and solving algebraic equations. Next it was PE, though.

Dodgeball

Fourth lesson was PE and it was dodgeball. I used my basketball practice to try and get everyone in our team back in by launching a long ranger into the hoop on the other side. There was just one other person and myself left, with their team full of players. Our backs were against the wall, so I went for it. Splash!

The bench erupted as everyone came hurtling back in. We went on to win the match, so the shot was not in vain.

Tutor Group

We got told today about specific details about the trip to the Highlands, as it was next Wednesday. This included behaviour, what to bring and what each day would look like.

Library lesson

Our last lesson of the day was an English lesson in the library, which I do like. It was an hour spent in the library with a bit more of a relaxed work ethic. That is the simplification of it. The outcry was huge after an English lesson in the library was replaced with an English lesson in the classroom instead. This was because our performance in an English lesson in the classroom (on the Friday last lesson) the week before was chaotic to say the least. Part of an English lesson in the Library was sitting on a massive sofa with great camaraderie and being at ease. We were usually set quite relaxing tasks that were therapeutic for our school experience because it was a time to enjoy being in a pleasant environment. Another outcry followed also, when we were informed that our library lesson had been cancelled, not because of behaviour but so that we could have another English lesson in the classroom was massive.

Basketball tournament

Robert and I were able to be excused early from the library lesson, to head to the minibus for the basketball tournament. When we arrived I was a bit concerned about the opposition because another team getting off the bus looked quite tough, but our team was up to it and beat them as it happened. The other team in the competition beat them as well. This meant that the final match between our team and the winners of the other match was basically the final. I got told I was on the bench by some of the keen players because I started the first one, so it was for rotation. However, the teacher intervened in team selection and all of a sudden I was starting. I enjoyed the close multiplayer combat battles of battling for a loose ball that had bounced off the hoop, with almost everyone crowding in to try and win the ball. I sunk a three pointer with my first shot of the match, after I found an opening. In the end, we actually won the match with a reasonable margin. We received a trophy, and who else would lift it apart from our 6ft 7 superstar. (This was another honour for the person, in addition to being taller than the rest of the school for the whole school photo. That was a nice moment for him in the past because it was in height order. So he was given a standing ovation when, as a year 8, he walked past year 9, 10 and 11's in the queue to the front of the line). Our triumph in the basketball tournament was quite funny actually because we won the Year 9 boys basketball tournament with a girl in our team. The organisers were kind enough not to disqualify us though.

Realities

Someone must have been annoyed with me today because they said I have no friends. For some reason it is common if someone is annoyed with you for whatever reason to say that you have no friends. I like to think that it isn't true in my case. Hopefully Patrick, Noah and Jonathan would back me up on that one. But even if it was true, there's no need to say it. Later in the day that very same person deliberately bashed my shoulder with theirs as I was walking down the corridor (the opposite way to them). It shows how negative school can get very quickly. The power of momentum, I suppose.

For example, it can sometimes look like teachers don't really show that they care about you and therefore make school actually a sad place to be because you feel that you're just dumped there. It occasionally appears that they just want you to turn up, be quiet and then go home. So it's important to keep a positive mind set and give constant reminders that all people are special, including ourselves.

Friday

Walk to school

On our walk to school today there was a tingle in the air because it was Friday. Someone was talking a lot about their life in geography, in our first lesson of the day, so much in fact that the person next to me said "no one cares". I don't know if they heard, but if they did, hopefully it did bring them back to down to earth.

RE

We then had RE which was nice because the teacher treats us well and also shows enthusiasm and enjoyment in his job. Thus, he would make lessons enjoyable, as was today's where he tried to do a trick with a football, which was interesting. This is because teachers are usually the ones telling students off for doing it, not actually taking part in it.

Food tech

After break time was food tech, and it was a practical, which was fantastic because it was part two of our current food creation, which was what people were first excited about when we heard about food tech at high school. It was the Chocolate Log! It is such a delicacy. Hence, it takes two lessons to fully complete. The first lesson was to make the log, and the second is to decorate it. When making the chocolate log, I found it quite difficult to crack the eggs on the edge of the bowl, in the first lesson. So I tried to use the table itself, but the eggs broke on the table. So I scooped the eggs off of the table and into the bowl with a spoon. After I finished decorating the log in today's lesson I put it onto the side counter at the back of the classroom to collect at the end of the day.

Fourth lesson

After we finished fourth lesson today, which was music, I breathed a sigh of relief. Now there was just lunchtime, tutor group and PE.

Friday lunch

Football wasn't on today, so it at least provided us with an opportunity to have something proper, with sustenance, for lunch. However, today was the day when everyone found out that the school canteen was offering takeaway fish and chips. This meant that as soon as it was our year group's turn for lunch there was the most compact scrum that I've been part of outside the canteen doors (and I'd been on a tube train at rush hour before). We'd been called down too early as well. Ah, now we had to wait in a scrum in order to enter the canteen. The assistant head teacher told us that we were being immature, but she didn't seem to understand that maturity gets thrown out of the window when takeaway fish and chips are on offer. I think some big kids in the year actually enjoyed dictating the scrum. This was probably what she was partly alluding to, because there was some quite aggressive pushing going on which made the experience of waiting, even more uncomfortable.

Although we couldn't play football on the astro, it didn't mean that we couldn't on the playground. So, after we tucked in to our fish and chips we played foot tennis by using our bags instead of a net, which made it easier for us. We decided that the winning team would stay on after a quick match of first to three points.

Tutor group was good today because it was another edition of the weekly Friday quiz and the teacher gave out sweets, which was appreciated. Friday quizzes are fabulous and a real highlight of the week, for me personally anyway. As I became more senior in the tutor group I gained more confidence to give my thoughts on what the answers were.

PE

Now that tutor group had ended it was PE and if I got to choose when the best time to have PE is, it would be Friday last lesson. As I didn't have my football boots; I thought that it would be best if I went with Boys Group 2. The alternative footwear I wore was... school shoes! It was better than the last time I did PE in my school shoes. This is because that time I forgot my whole PE kit and played in a small pair of joggers, a rugby shirt and my school shoes, as a result. There was some real positivity in the changing room today which was nice to see. I was very happy to see this positive attitude. Attitude really does have the ability to dictate the mood of an atmosphere, I find. It was going to be a two thirds football match with full size goals, so the Boys Group 1 could play a small match on the final third of the astro turf. The PE teacher understood that we just wanted to play football, and weren't interested in any of the drills nonsense. What was really nice, was when we put on the bibs. They were dry! It turns out they were brand new, so they weren't wet with rain or sweat but they were actually quite pleasant to wear. In the first half I fancied scoring some goals so I went in attack but I kept on missing so I demoted myself to defence because our team didn't deserve my finishing in attack. While I was defending, the sense of achievement from doing two blocks in quick succession was highly satisfying, as were the high fives that came with it. As the match appeared to be drifting towards a 0-0,

Jordan tossed the ball up fields towards Jonathan. It was a bouncing ball and Jonathan got ahead of it and held his man off, to shield the ball. Then he fell backwards, using all of his backward momentum to kick the ball with enough pace so that it could reach the goal. It was like slow motion, the ball was trickling past people towards goal, before it eventually found the side netting, beating the goalkeeper. Madness ensued! Our team was in awe of the creativity of the goal. What a way for a 1-0 to be decided, amid the only goal to be scored in the whole match, as the match ended shortly as 1-0. Everyone piled on top of Jonathan and it was definitely the biggest pile on I've been part of because it was pretty painful and I wasn't even at the bottom.

Friday Night

Tonight was Friday night and Noah was kind enough to host a games night. Now when I say games, yes I do mean computer games. But we say Friday night only. What we do is a career mode and every Friday evening we do a part of the football season. We did this after playing football at Noah's family's orchard, which was very therapeutic indeed. In the cup final, Noah came up with a late winner so of course there was a fabulous pile on and was thankfully less painful than the one in PE. This is a real bonus of computer games: none of us have to run to the pile on. On this occasion Patrick, Jonathan and I piled onto the match winner straight away.

Wednesday

Leaving for sleeper train to Inverness

I have had a break from writing to rest and prepare for the Highlands trip, so tonight is the following Wednesday night from when I last wrote. As we were going to be getting the sleeper train tonight, I acknowledged before I left home that it would be an extended period of time before I returned, so I enjoyed the last moments before leaving because there is no place like home. We were able to choose rooming options so Noah, Patrick, Jonathan and I would all be in the same cabin on the train and room at the Geography Retreat Centre in the Highlands. We each valued the importance of loyalty.

It was a funny feeling arriving at school at 6pm because for other trips we were usually there early in the morning rather being there for the evening, but I suppose it was because we were getting the night train. Everyone was very excited for the upcoming residential to the Highlands. It would give us a real chance to have a glimpse of what being away from home for a while, would be like because this was the longest school residential trip any of us students had been on.

I wondered whether this trip would go a bit smoother than my last school residential to Continental Europe. On that trip some people forgot to say that they were vegetarian, so it was a bit awkward when the only option was meat, in the evening of the first day. Then, that same evening we went bowling and I left the bowling alley with my bowling shoes on. I only noticed on the road by the bus and the teacher was furious so I quickly ran back and swapped them for my shoes. Then, later that night I got hit by a packet of crisps out of nowhere.

So, back to the Highlands trip, while we met in the school car park we saw that Robert looked absolutely exhausted, and it turns out he had flown in that morning from Kerala, arriving back in England at midday. Now that is commitment. But, did he look fresh? There must be something about going away that is very beneficial to a person, and I suppose Kerala as well. I hadn't seen someone who looked as refreshed as him for a long time. I suppose a school residential has opportunity for exciting times and a bit of team bonding as well. So people like to attend them if possible, hence a sleep-deprived Robert had decided to come along.

Sleeper Train Day 1

We boarded the sleeper train. It was nice because the teachers didn't have access to our rooms so we were able to relax, knowing that they wouldn't burst in when we were getting changed. Some may say that it would've been better to fly to Inverness because it is faster.

But by going on a sleeper train there is the advantage to look outside and see how the scenery changes through England and into Scotland. Furthermore, it allowed more time for camaraderie on the journey, which is valuable in life, I find. It was a great setting to a have a therapeutic and joyful experience of being with friends from school in a more relaxed environment. In our cabin we had two bunk beds, so none of us would have to double up, which was nice.

Quiz Day 1

On the train there was also a big conference room, where Mr Filey had created a quiz for the evening. The four of us came up with the team name ... 'The Team from the Shire'. The quiz had four topics, sport, geography, history and the Highlands. We came second, with another team pipping us by a couple of points, but we had given our all, so we weren't disappointed. The quiz was interesting though because I had an interest in the four topics. But, to wet our appetites some more there was another challenge that evening ...

Message Day 1

All dotted around the train, there were pictures taped to the wall. We were told by Mr Cambridge we had to decipher a message out of the sheets of paper. The winner would win a mystery prize. The first picture showed a golf flag on a green which was relevant because we were heading to Scotland, the home of golf. The next picture was of a boat drifting around the coast of

Monaco. How did we know it was Monaco? There were five racing drivers on the boat. Following on from this there was a picture of a man saying hello in French, with a speech bubble coming out of his mouth to signal this. After was an image of Will Patch, the all-star racing driver from the Highlands. Then, simply a picture of a single @ followed on. Further down was an image with a cinema screen, with the credits listed. In the next carriage a picture was, bizarrely, of a person not catching what someone else had said. In addition, was a picture of a muddy sign displaying a cycling event. Furthermore, there was a picture showing seven pairs of socks with a day on each pair from Monday to Sunday. The final picture appeared to have some sort of insect on it. Even though this was an individual task the four of us were stumped. How could all of these pictures make a message? Discussions went on for about half an hour. Suddenly, Noah called "Bingo." We thought he must have been impulsive and become bored of the impasse. Mr Cambridge asked Noah why he called out 'Bingo' because he was implying that he wasn't expecting anyone to get close to completing this challenge and Noah responded that he thought that was the right word to gather attention to the fact that he had deciphered the message. Everyone nodded in agreement as well as Mr Cambridge. After a pause of anticipation, Noah then announced "We will be at a flagship event this weekend". Our jaws dropped! Mr Cambridge dropped his flask. Thankfully it was empty. We had something to be excited for. But, how had Noah worked that out from the pictures? The prize Noah won was a Barbeque chicken pizza. Mr Cambridge then announced that it was the curfew for all of us to return to our cabins for the night. Feeling triumphant that one of our pals had won the main event of the evening we went into our cabin quite chuffed. Noah, being such a gentlemen, shared his prize with us in the cabin. It was a real meal, very tasty, very sweet.

Cabin Day 1

It was quite funny being in a cabin with friends from school on a moving train. We had a conversation on how this time last year we wouldn't have imagined being together in this current setting. But because we all recognise the importance of sleep we did soon turn in afterwards. I do think the excitement of being away from home led to our two neighbours being quite loud. It was a funny experience trying to get to sleep while lying down on a train. It added a unique aspect to the trip.

Morning Day 2

We woke up at 7am, and were able to order breakfast to our cabin. As we needed energy for a big day ahead, we thought we'd each order a full English breakfast. But then Noah suddenly said that other people probably wouldn't have ordered breakfast yet so the conference room would probably be empty. So we got ready, and then headed to the conference room.

Just as Noah thought, there was no one else in there, so we ordered our breakfasts there. This is why it is a gift that we share the Earth with other people because they can come up with ideas that we don't think of.

Mr Cambridge Day 2
==================

A few minutes later Mr Cambridge came in and asked if he could join us, to which we replied "of course." The thing with a student - teacher relationship is that it is different to a normal relationship, because they have authority over you. Hence, if you're trying to be friends with a teacher and then you're late to their lesson for example, it is very awkward when they tell you off. So we didn't try to be friends with Mr Cambridge, even though we were in a relaxed environment. Mr Cambridge told us this story about when he was younger he saved a penalty in the last minute of extra time to take the match to penalties and then saved three out of three penalties in the shootout to win the cup final for his school. It was also interesting to see the big difference between England and Scotland when looking out of the window. As anticipated the sleeper train had provided the opportunity to have a nice comparison between the two countries and their landscapes, as we travelled along. What is nice about a residential school trip for both students and teachers is that it mixes things up, and provides time for a bit of a change and refresh. It was already proving to be this way early on in the trip less than a full day in. This is because Mr Cambridge was being more open in this new environment. We also had teas with our breakfast which perked us up quite nicely, and was also quite civilised if I may say so. It was very peaceful in the conference room, thus making it an enjoyable place to sit in and eat our breakfasts.

After breakfast Day 2

After we finished our breakfast, we stayed in the conference room to have discussions about various subjects to become more enriched in our knowledge and understanding of different topics, in the hope of becoming more well-rounded people. Soon other pupils piled in from their rooms, although some had opted to eat breakfast in their cabins. So I suppose other students had come in because it was more spacious. It was still a while to go until Inverness and the rest of the journey was rather restful, seeing us breeze past the Scottish Countryside.

Inverness Day 2

We eventually arrived in Inverness, much to everyone's excitement to step foot in Scotland. This is because for most of us, it would be the first time. After leaving the train station we all boarded the coach. Then it was a relatively quick coach trip to Ullapool. As were travelling by we saw a golf course. Wow, what a spectacle; lush, green nature. Amazing! To cap it all off, a golfer did a fantastic iron shot onto the green. Fabulous to see the wonders of creation, how special people are and what they are capable of.

The activity for the morning was exploring Ullapool, and dissecting different parts of its urban geographical data into tables, while walking through the town. We must have stuck out like sore thumbs to the people of Ullapool, being a bunch of English schoolchildren in normal clothes walking around with clipboards, during school hours.

Calculating Waves Day 2

While our group was in the middle of measuring the size and shape of different pebbles on the beach at the edge of the sea, Jeremy suddenly pushed me, before Clive benched me right into the water. I was now all soaked from Jeremy and Clive who are given the most authority in the year, for some reason, even though they can be quite cruel. A teacher rushed over, and asked me if I needed a new sheet, not whether I would like to get changed but just about whether I could still record data. Let's not forget this was the west coast of the Highlands, so it was pretty cold. It was a chance to be a champion and power through the pain barrier though. But it also allowed me to learn a lesson of the real world that not everyone will look to help you. Once we finished the task, we then headed to the centre on the coach.

Geography Retreat Centre Day 2 evening

When we arrived at the centre I was impressed by how clean the bathrooms were. They were spic and span. When we got into our allocated room, we thought this'll do nicely. But we first had to set up for sleeping which was something that we were completely unprepared for. Thankfully, Jonathan is quite practical, so he was able to give us a hand, to get everything sorted such as the duvet cover.

Football pitch Day 2

At the centre, there was a little football pitch so we had a little bit of headers and volleys action.

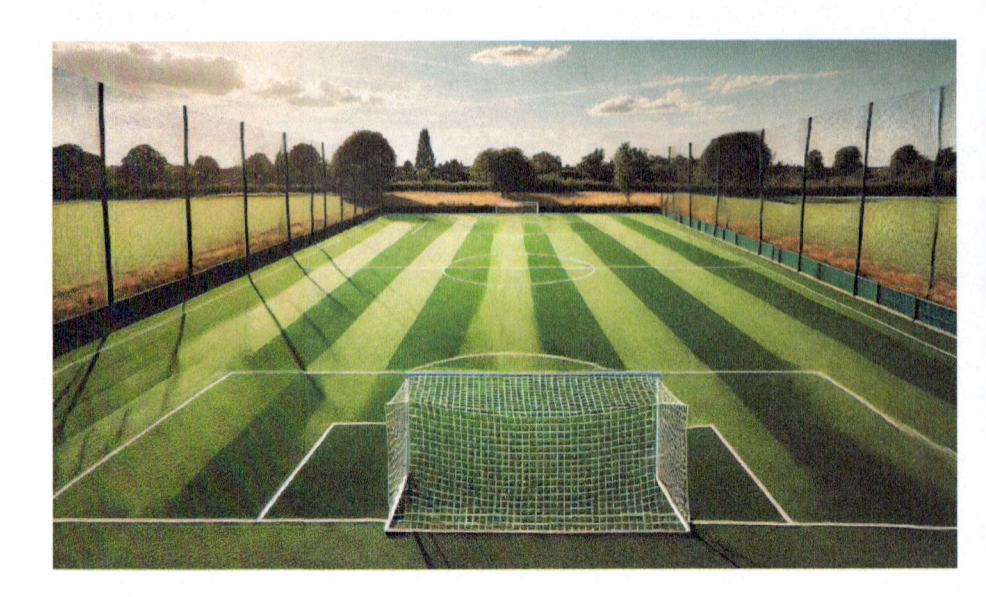

I saw some people who weren't using their hands in goal early on but when there was only one goal left they were diving all over the place, out of desperation, in an attempt to not risk being painfully punished. We also played a small match but towards the end, some people were being mischievous and out of nowhere I was benched, with others also having this done to them. It wasn't a pleasant experience being benched twice in one day.

Patrol Day 2 - 3

The Centre announced before the curfew that students had to help with security patrols at night. One member of accommodation staff would be on it and then four students would help. It was quite nice actually, as well as also being refreshing and therapeutic. Patrick, Noah, Jonathan and I were chosen for the first night. When Patrick and I were in the off-duty hut, after our first watch (which was uneventful) we broke out a board game and it was great fun. As we were sort of working for the Centre we were allowed unlimited, free hot drinks. This was a nice gesture from the Centre and made the board game in the hut even more enjoyable. Also there were plates of chocolate biscuits, but it was hard to get the balance right between making the most of the opportunity but also not being greedy. It was quite nice that there was a TV in the hut because that was something to occupy ourselves with nicely after playing a board game. We had been given responsibility and the door was open before our eyes of what the real world looked like. There was an opportunity for the four of us to bond and have comradeship by looking out for each other. This was a time when we were all equals and there was no one who was better than someone else because we were still schoolkids. It was also nice to have a sense that we were doing something worthwhile and important for other people. It was on our second stint of duty that we noticed a shadow in the trees, and when we realised that the shadow was the shape of a person, we called out... "Turn out the Guard! Turn out the Guard!" Now we had everyone available on the case. It turns out that it was just a local, who said that they'd missed the last train and was trying to find somewhere among the trees to sleep. As one of the Centre staff was on guard with us he said they had a spare room in the Centre that he could have for the night. Now that the situation was under control, Patrick and I agreed how fun it was calling 'Turn out the Guard'. While, Noah, Jonathan and the member of the Geography Retreat Centre staff who were off duty (in the hut) said how exciting it was to be called out like they were the cavalry coming to the rescue. We were all honest enough to admit that it was quite nerve racking at first, when we didn't know what we were dealing with. Incidentally, we did see foxes quite often during the night and they were quite cunning, but we had safety in numbers, especially with our no fear attitude. Overall, there wasn't really much going on around the property. I'm glad that we remembered to bring our coats with us (from England) because we certainly needed them that night. The hut was nice and warm so we were able to take our coats off and relax when we were relieved. It was nice seeing the sun rise, when it did, because we knew that our work had been done. Also it was the end of our only night post of the week, so now we were all free to sleep during the nights for the rest of the trip.

Full kit breakfast Day 3

Someone turned up to breakfast in a full England kit, with shin pads! For the second time on this trip, our jaws had dropped. It was weird having cereal with other people who I only usually eat sandwiches and crisps with on weekday lunchtimes.

Our first geography activity of the day was to measure the gradient of the beach. As it was the start of the day we were excited about doing the task, so there was a lot of energy. We got on and did it across different checkpoints along a one kilometre distance, to give comparisons and an average gradient along this one kilometre section of the beach.

Corn beef lunch Day 3
===

Lunchtime wasn't at the Centre, so we were given a bit more freedom with that. We decided to pop to a corner shop and combine brioche buns and corn beef together to make a rather unconventional, but still fabulous lunch.

Someone else bought a single pint of milk and received hostile abuse, as a result. But, I really respected this person for purchasing and consuming what they wanted and not taking notice of other people's thoughts or opinions. I bought myself a 1.5 litre bottle of water, which came under scrutiny because of its large size, which one person saw as unnecessary. But, they then asked me to pour some water into their water bottle. This justified my decision quite nicely I thought, at least it did to myself. What was funny is that when I was younger I always thought that when I was older I would have complete freedom in a shop to purchase whatever I like and that I would get stuck in. But now that I was older and the opportunity had presented itself, I realised that it wasn't sensible and I didn't end up buying all of the items that I thought I would, when I was younger.

Basketball competition Day 3

We decided to eat our lunch on the sand by the sea, to make the most of our surroundings because we live quite far inland in England, so seeing the sea is a luxury for us. After we'd all finished our lunch we saw a sports hall entrance, with a sign outside that read 'Hit five consecutive three pointers to win a trip to Herzegovina and a year's supply of Belgian Buns'. I noticed out of the corner of my eye, Noah's eyes lit up when he saw the words 'Belgian Buns', on the sign. Hence, as soon as Noah entered the sports hall he asked the organiser what kind of Belgian Buns were part of the prize. The event was free because Travel Herzegovina and Brilliant Belgian Buns were both sponsoring the event. It may have sounded like it wasn't very hard but we saw elite challengers hit four and then crumble on the fifth when the pressure ramped up and miss. That is the power of pressure.

Patrick Day 3

Patrick was the last up, and no one was really watching at this point, as the three of us beforehand had each missed our first go. But, as Patrick was scoring his way around the three point line, with the ball doing anything but swishing, more heads were turning his way. Patrick just needed one more to win the prize. The pressure had built up; all eyes were now on Patrick and the basketball he was holding in his hands. He went for it! Noah, Jonathan and I were behind Patrick ready to catch him, in case he made it and fell back like a champion. The trajectory was looking good... and it was a... swish! The hall erupted! Patrick fell back onto us, and we caught him before he was swallowed up. People piled in to make a very packed scrummage around Patrick, to try and get a glimpse of the man. It was fabulous to be in the middle of such an amazing aftermath.

After Patrick gave the Belgian Buns rep his address for the deliveries and also gave the travel company his email address, we all went to the meeting point.

Groynes Day 3 Afternoon

The afternoon session was measuring the build-up of sediment on each side of the ten groynes that were on the beach.

At least we were outside. This was one of those tasks where you just have to get on with the job. But it was really nice again just to be next to the sea. While we were focusing on the data collection, we noticed that the racing world champion, Paul Justice, was having a paddle. We thought it was funny seeing him in his own clothes rather than in his team gear. We thought it was the perfect opportunity to gain some go-karting tips off the master, so we asked. He was very kind and generous with his time, considering that we were all strangers. Maybe that's because we weren't chasing him or putting our arms around him for pictures without asking. We asked him if he wouldn't mind being in a picture with us in front of the sea, and he kindly obliged, with a nice natural smile for the take. After we had collected the data from the first ten groynes on the beach we all headed back to the coach and journeyed back to the centre.

Viral clip Day 3 Evening

When we got back to the centre, James (pronounced Hamez, because he's from Columbia), showed us that someone had filmed Patrick's hero run and that the clip had gone viral. He also told us that high school basketball teams, in America, were now after Patrick. Did the aftermath look wild from the outside; it was exactly how it was from my eyes when I was there. The amazing achievement by Patrick was certainly given the celebrations it deserved. Seeing ourselves in a viral video was unusual because many times before we'd seen people we didn't know in them, but not this time. We were given deep fried beef, deep fried chips, and deep fried peas for dinner. It was delicious. Not sure about nutritious, but everything in moderation, I suppose. After that was a deep fried brownie.

Cinema evening Day 3

This evening in Scotland we were given the treat of going to the cinema. We went to watch 'The Warriors of Football'.

It was about this group of boys who had one star player, but the overall team had a fantastic attitude and gave absolutely everything when they played, with good unity. Their coach said that they had to squeeze the most out of their ability. The game plan was to try and get one goal and then shield their own goal with their whole team at a high intensity, with bravery and courage. It showed in the first round the front four targeting the right wing, with the star man guiding it along in this direction of play before he darted into the box and the ball bobbled into his path, from the right side by one of the other four attackers, and he finished it into the bottom left-corner past the goalkeeper. Then there was a defensive masterclass by the team to win 1-0. The changing room scenes afterwards were full of joy. You could sense that the whole audience was enjoying a very refreshing film that shows what attitude and loyalty can achieve with 100% effort.

To display rounds two, three and four the film then showed a montage of great defensive displays, the sight of work on the players' faces and the main match highlights as they were all 0-0 and then won on penalties. I assume that the film production probably wanted to save their money and time for the semi final and final.

In the semi final, the team played a good side and so planned to protect their goal and then win on penalties, unless they could score somehow. The match was very absorbing to see all of the last-ditch tackles, goal line clearances and blocks from players throwing themselves at the ball. Then towards the end of the match, the coach called for the long ball. All of a sudden the players darted up the pitch and the goalkeeper did something that is commonly known to kids in England, as a 'big kick'. The players made a line of steel to guard the opposition against the bouncing ball and the star man before he, after the football bounced up to a nice height, hit the ball sweetly with his laces into the top corner before the ref blew for the final whistle to end the match. The pile on after the match was superb.

In the final it was awesome to see a team talk in the cinema about a genre of film that I am in the target market of. It was a real motivational speech, but it also had sustenance to it. (He quoted Beethoven; 'to play the wrong note is insignificant; to play without passion is inexcusable.') It was a continuation of getting stuck in and defending as a team by getting in the way of the goal almost instantly, with hunger and desire. The final went into extra time. The left back had managed to charge forward and the ball was cut back to him on the edge of the box. He hit the ball with his laces into the crossbar, down to the ground and then back up to bulge the roof of the net to score the golden goal and win the final for his team. The mayhem of the celebrations was fabulous to see. There was pure joy, rather than there being any selfishness of an individual player, with the team celebrating together. Everyone charged towards the match winner to join the pile on, after they slid into the corner flag. What a sight, seeing a team that had given everything, triumph over teams with more skilful players to win the Cup. It was a very good moral for life, I thought.

After the film we were inspired with a newfound energy; showing that making the most of what you have, can be a formidable force. We also learned how embracing a challenge can be quite an exciting adventure.

Games room Day 3 evening

We arrived back to the Centre by coach, and then went into the games room. Patrick was busy playing table tennis against Robert, so Noah and I needed another opponent as well as Jonathan to play table football against. And so entered Mr Cambridge! He had obviously read between the lines that we needed another player. As it was a school trip, there was a curfew to be in our rooms by 10 pm, which I thought was fair. So after Mr Cambridge and Jonathan won 9-8, it was time to head upstairs. However, there was talking outside our door at 2am according to my watch, which woke all of us up. We were all thinking the same thing and gathered behind the door so that if entry was obtained we could take the intruder down. The door opened. It was an orthodox take down by the four of us. It was Jeremy; I am guessing that he was planning some sort of dastardly act while we were asleep. We made it clear to him that we didn't approve of his behaviour, and then he left.

Midnight feast Day 3-4

We fancied a classic and maybe slightly cringe midnight feast so we thought we'd enjoy some Belgian Buns in the canteen of the centre we were staying at. Then we heard footsteps… Mr Cambridge and Mr Filey were heading towards the scene. We scarpered. We ran down the corridor into the games room, where we were cornered. We all decided to hide behind the door. As they came in they turned the lights on. We put our hoods up and turned and ran back to our room, then we took our hoodies off and hid them, before turning the lights off. We heard doors being opened and closed nearby, and then Mr Cambridge and Mr Filey opened the door before shortly closing it again because they saw that we were settled, in a sleeping position. After about fifteen minutes of being back in the room we heard a smash and so went next door to find out that a glass had broken. They'd been messing around with a football which had deflected off a wall and smashed a glass onto a bedside table. It had been quite an eventful night, but we did shortly get to sleep after.

Flagship event breakfast discussion Day 4

The next morning it was cereal again for breakfast, and there was a discussion about what surprise activity we would be doing this weekend. Noah said he thought we'd be going to the Scottish Grand Prix. Robert said to Noah that he was getting into the realms of fantasy because tickets had been sold out for months and they were very expensive. Then Mr Filey walked in with a racing jumper on and announced that we'd be attending the Scottish Grand Prix on Sunday. Credit to Noah, he wasn't smug and instead carried on eating his cereal, as normal. This morning we were told to meet in the outdoor classroom that was detached from the main centre.

It was a funny feeling being in a classroom on a Saturday morning, but we made ourselves comfortable and listened to the group leader. We were told by the group leader that we would collect sand dune data and visit another town in the day ahead.

Sand Dunes lecture Day 4 morning

52

We were taken to the sand dunes and were given a lecture on the beach about sand dunes, in front of them. Very appropriate I thought. We then had to collect various pieces of data, deep into the sand dunes. We had to measure the pH and moisture level of the soil, which was simple by using the metre for each one individually. But measuring the angle change was quite difficult at times because occasionally we'd measure different angles to each other when we each used the clinometer. Our dignity could also feel the strain at times when we had to be in awkward poses by putting our feet on something substantial, in order to look through the clinometer. The things we do to maximise our potential of success in a task.

Smoked Salmon lunch day 4

For lunch today, we all went to the supermarket and saw some smoked salmon on offer, and all looked at each other and nodded. We purchased some basil also, as well as four pink lady apples (one each) and also a large French Baguette that could be broken into four. Of course we also had some Belgian Buns to sink our teeth into, kindly provided by Patrick. The same sports hall we went into yesterday was having another competition. This time it was that a group of four people must all hit the crossbar consecutively. We wondered whether it would be a year's supply of Iced Fingers and a trip to France for the prize. We walked in, and it turns out that it was a year's supply of Hot Cross Buns and a trip to Portugal. Noah said he had another important question to ask, so he walked up to the Hot Cross Bun rep and asked what type they were. The rep responded "the ordinary type". We waited our turn, but today's challenge was a lot harder than yesterday and most teams were struggling to complete the first strike.

Our turn in Crossbar Event Day 4 Early Afternoon

Our turn had arrived, so we all took our jumpers off, to prevent any unnecessary air resistance disrupting our run up and connection with the football. Noah did a very nice floater onto the crossbar, to start off. Patrick stepped up and went for a curler onto the crossbar and again, it was very nice. Now it was my go. I just wanted to give us a chance of hitting the jackpot. At this point, eyes were starting to become more focused on us. Like Noah I also went for a floater and the crossbar was hit. Now all eyes were on Jonathan. Could he do it? He chipped it. The place fell silent. Many pairs of eyes were now tracking the ball and it … skimmed the crossbar! He had done it! The three of us piled into Jonathan and the crowd followed in with mayhem unfolding. But the official announced through a megaphone that it hadn't hit. Everyone froze! Jonathan was sure it had hit, so the three of us were hopeful. The replay was played on the big screen in slow motion to see whether we would be eating Hot Cross Buns in Portugal. The replay showed the ball travelling towards the crossbar and there was … a definite skim. As there'd been some adversity and tension in our accomplishment, the mayhem in the celebrations was even bigger this time round. We'd had our joy snatched away but we then had snatched it back, to make the whole sequence of events, even sweeter. The four of us were all of a sudden swallowed up. It was hard to comprehend that everyone was crowding around us in the Highlands of all places, when we are from England, which made it quite thrilling.

Dingwall Day 4 afternoon

The afternoon session was filling in questionnaires in Dingwall High Street. This could be a challenge at times because we had to try and talk to complete strangers. Then Noah suggested that a charity shop worker may perhaps be more open to filling in the questionnaire. He was right; they were willing to answer the questionnaire, very courteous and very positive.

Day 4 evening classroom

That evening we were in the classroom to plan our project to carry out in the summer by ourselves. I think because it was a Saturday, productivity suffered and various random subjects were being discussed. This put everyone in quite a jovial mood, as a matter of fact. We respected being in the classroom, but it appeared that unanimously without any discussion everyone had sort of decided between themselves to make the classroom time enjoyable, fuelled by the exhaustion that we were all carrying. Sometimes by people not trying to be hysterical, they could be and that is I suppose what made it quite a lively evening. Someone decided to ask Mr Filey the awkward question about the finances of teachers coming on the trp. He responded by saying that they don't get paid to come on the trip. The student did say that they get to go for free, though. To be fair to teachers they are responsible for a group of kids. So, I wouldn't really call it a free vacation, but they still seemed to be excited for the Grand Prix, tomorrow.

Day 4 games room and lounge

There was still time afterwards for us to spend in the games room. Today we decided to do doubles on the table tennis. But there was also another school at the centre, now, which added an extra dynamic to the trip.

There was also a lounge, so we watched a couple of episodes of a series about a fictional road mender crew and their daily activities.

Patrick is very open to sharing and offered us some Belgian Buns as soon as he pulled them out of his bag. Unlike most theme openings we really enjoyed the one on this programme because it was quite enjoyable and was part of the excitement building up to the episode. After the second episode finished it was the curfew, but we were told to clear away all of the crumbs from the Belgian Buns, first by Mr Filey.

Day 4 evening noise and intrusion

The other school was making an absolute racket, with their noise, that isn't worthy of being called music. So some students from our school were stomping their feet on the floor to make them stop. Then one student, who had their own little side room, had one of the other school's teachers burst in. Thankfully he was in a respectful state, but he was a bit surprised at what happened.

Sunday morning Day 5 of the trip

We woke up to a Sunday morning and as we are a Catholic school, we attended Mass. After Mass, Mr Cambridge gave all of us a bottle of water to drink. After we all drank some water, he said we had an hour and a half at the seaside before we would head to the Grand Prix. It was quite pleasant to be by the sea, after having gone to Mass.

Beach cricket Day 5 morning

With our free time some of us decided to play cricket because Jonathan had brought a bat and a ball from England. We then fetched three sticks and dug them into the sand for stumps. At our age and level of interest we just tried to slog the ball into the leg side. That was pretty much our only shot selection because we were just interested in having fun. As other students fancied a bit of cricket, there were plenty of fielders. As all batsmen were going for it, the fielders were given a lot of opportunities for action. Patrick again was the sporting superstar, being the only person to hit the ball into the sea.

Another highlight was when Jonathan bowled and knocked the middle stick out of the sand thanks to the ball having an incredibly low bounce and sneaking under Noah's bat.

Unorthodox lunch Day 5

For lunch we had premium cheese in brioche buns, which may sound unorthodox, but it was nice. This was because if we were going to be champions we'd have to be unorthodox. We thought we'd have our lunch on a bench overlooking the sea to make the most of being near it.

The Scottish Grand Prix Day 5

The time did come to head to the Highlands Speed Machine (the name of the circuit). The Scottish Grand Prix, in the Highlands, now awaited us. A purpose built race track, next to the sea. Fabulous! I do wonder if Mr Cambridge, who organised this trip, had the grand prix in mind when he chose the dates for this trip because he was wearing full merchandise of Paul Justice. Obviously, we weren't going to complain because who doesn't like a bit of high-speed action.

It was a wonderful landscape for racing; it's also nice that Britain were given a second grand prix because, I suppose I'm British, and biased. Being school children, the circuit gave the school a huge discount for our tickets. A nice gesture, indeed, from the circuit staff.

Paddock Day 5

We went into the paddock, with some students from our school trying to gain new screen savers. It was about how brave they were feeling, and whether they were willing to risk their dignity by being rejected by drivers for pictures. Paul Justice was doing a pre-race interview with Sidney Sports, when Clive dive bombed the interview and got a snapshot, with Paul Justice, before the presenter nudged him out of the way, as softly as they could, in an attempt to not appear like a brute in front of their viewers. Some people appear to have less boundaries than others. Then afterwards some people decided to get in shot of the TV coverage of Sidney Sports later and mess about in the back drop.

Our view was brilliant because it showed the breaking zone after a long straight (that was useful for overtaking) before a slow left corner, into a small straight and then a fast left hander afterwards. In the penultimate lap of the race Paul Justice was going alongside William Patch into the braking zone after the long straight. Justice then danced around the outside to take the lead: he had more traction coming out of the corner, allowing him to take the lead. The speed through the corners was awe-inspiring.

So, a couple of laps later we saw Justice parading around on his victory lap, after keeping Patch behind for the victory. We then raced onto the track (pun) to watch the podium ceremony.

After the race we were given some free time to stroll down the Bay of Ardmair, a hidden gem.

Day 6 morning

This next morning we awoke at 4am because Clive next door said he must've accidentally swiped the alarm on for this time. Some people were more bothered than others and there was prevention taken to stop some from losing their tempers, and the whole affair boiling over. Thankfully, harmony was restored and we all went back to sleep. We woke up at a more suitable time on the next occasion, with some time to freshen up before breakfast.

Day 6 morning measuring wave strength

This morning we were measuring the strength of the waves so we had to throw a tennis ball into the sea at various points along the coast to measure the strength of the waves. The issue was that it may have been missed out in the risk assessment, the danger of giving some people tennis balls. The teachers saw this as a time to rest so they left us to it and supervised from a distance. Hence, Jeremy and Clive started throwing tennis balls, after they'd soaked them in the water to make them even harder. So there was a tennis ball throwing scene that I was caught in the middle of. Mr Cambridge came over and ordered us to break it up and stop these shenanigans. In order to do this Mr Cambridge asked Jonathan to hold his flask of tea but the lid wasn't on properly, so Jonathan didn't make an effort to hold it upright. As a result the flask was drained and when Mr Cambridge retrieved his tea he thought Jonathan had drank it. Their faces were a picture. Now that's my sort of humour.

Fish and Chips lunch Day 6

For lunch today we had fish and chips... from the fish and chip shop. We saw a deal that was amazing value, so we capitalised. After we had finished eating, we saw a boating lake and still had some time left of our lunch break; so we thought why not.

We went for two rowing boats, and it was quite pleasant. We thought to ourselves that this trip was providing all sorts of opportunities for different activities.

The afternoon session was some more coastal data collecting. It was comparing the effectiveness of different examples of soft and hard engineering. We would then have to evaluate each by noting down the benefits and drawbacks of each one.

Day 6 evening Waterpark

Tonight we were told once we got back to the centre that we would be going to a waterpark. Oh yes! It was indeed high fives all round. We had all assumed that when it said to bring our swimming costume, on the kit list, it was a punishment for a student to swim late at night in the sea by themselves, with the shame of the rest of school watching. Or that it was, as a school we were going to be toughened up and thrown into the sea and forced to swim in the artic water temperatures in the evening, after the sun had gone down. We arrived at the waterpark and went into the locker rooms. The first thing was to see if there were any cubicles to get changed in because I wasn't going anywhere near the public gallery changing areas. That isn't their proper name but is sort of what they are. Thankfully there were plenty of cubicles available. We soon got changed, showered and then headed into the unknown.

There was a waterslide in view straight away so Jonathan, Patrick, Noah and I all over walked to it. Ah. We hadn't anticipated there would be such a big queue. That's the thing with exciting activities, you usually assume that there will be perfect conditions when you're and then it's a bit different when you actually get there. So we thought we'd go over to the wave machine, while others had the early excitement to go on the slide, and then use it after their excitement had faded and the queue had become smaller.

The wave machine was good fun, because it created something to be active against because I didn't want to be defeated by the wave and go underneath it. Still, I don't think it matched the speed of the slide, so when we saw the queue was smaller, we set out on the first steps of our adventure.

The slide Day 6 evening

The slide was fabulous, but Jeremy decided to go straight in after the four of us with a run up as he hopped, with momentum, into the slide, and as the last of the four of us (myself) had completed the journey into the little pool after the exit of the slide there was a crash. Jeremy went straight into the back of me which created a dented effect until Patrick at the front was collided against. Thankfully we were all OK, except our dignity. But then, we all looked up at the gigantic waterslide and thought shall we? We thought it looked like it would be very exhilarating and of course we weren't fearful. Some people went up to the top of the slide and then screamed and left, with some choosing not to go up at all.

As we were walking up to the top of the slide a few students were slowly getting into the big waterslide because they appeared to be measured in how they would approach going down the slide. But then suddenly a member of the public gave the person at the back a massive push, just as they were slowly getting themselves ready to launch catching them off-guard.

We reached the entrance to the slide, after quite an upwards trek. Then we thought whether this was such a good idea when we looked down. But, we decided to go for it, and plunged into the deep end. Now there was no going back. We had committed to an adventure inside of an adventure (the trip to the Highlands). I was told by Robert before we did go big or go home that apparently Jeremy had had to hold Clive's hand; he got so frightened when they went on this slide. This was just to warn me about how terrifying the slide might actually be. The first bend was so fast that my shoulder took a wack against the wall for its troubles. As we were going so fast, we weren't able to react or prepare for what might lie ahead. We were literally passengers for what was coming for us. We just had to try and brace ourselves and be ready for anything that might lie ahead or that the waterslide could throw at us. There's not much else to say, but that it was very fast, and took no account for braking. We just hoped that we could adjust ourselves in time to make each corner cleanly. We saw light and started to relax, until we realised that the waterslide ends by tossing you into the air. Then we all just managed to catch Noah say "it's a big drop". The sensation of being tossed into the air with my buddies was awesome and it was quite exciting, including the bracing for impact of the water. Thankfully, the water was quite deep so we didn't hit the bottom after landing.

Day 6 Waterpark basketball hoop

This waterpark was different to your average one because it had a basketball hoop, and all through the evening there were many long shots. It was so hard to get it in from such a distance, so they were all misses, until... Robert projected 'mira y aprende' and launched the ball as he was tossed into the air off the tallest waterslide. And swish! Robert lifted his head above the surface to quite a roar! The waterpark loved it because finally someone had done it and was it awesome. There were many splashes in the pool, as everyone swam over to Robert, trying to congratulate him.

After we left and entered the shower area, some people thought that it was droll to squirt their shampoo at other people, but being covered in various different liquids is not my idea of fun. There was no teacher to supervise us, so I wonder whether that was what sparked this sudden, random behaviour. We all got changed pretty quickly after that just so we could get back onto the coach and to safety.

When we got back to the Centre it was very nice, because we'd earnt our rest after our antics down at the waterpark.

Day 7 morning Ferry

The next morning it was the Ferry day, where we would be crossing into the Hebrides, to visit Iona. We were prepped that it was going to be a long day but it was a nice touch from the school, to do this visit today. This is because it wasn't part of our data collection practise for our project, but it was just a good day trip. The Scottish, at the Centre, were very kind and gave us a full English breakfast this morning, which went down well. We all loaded up the coach to head off to the port. Once we reached the port we then boarded the ferry to the Isle of Mull.

After docking we then carried on through Mull before boarding another ferry to Iona. The ferries were more enjoyable than the coach because it was on the water and you could move around on board, because they were quite large. As soon as we stepped foot on Iona, there was something different about the air. The teachers had said the long travels would be worth it and it sure was. Of course, we first visited Iona Abbey which was very spiritual. St Columbia's bay was very nice, especially with the fabulous view. But visiting all of the sites, and experiencing them along with the island as a whole was truly special. We were all quite tired after our long, but amazing day, and the return journey to the Centre breezed by.

Day 7 Football

That evening we had a bit more headers and volleys action, but after someone had ended up in goal and was therefore likely going to have to face some punishment, they suddenly said they had something else to do. Very convenient. We weren't going to let him off that easily. There was plenty of audible pain as people were toughened up, that evening. There were many ways for oneself to be put in the firing line. Being in goal at the end was one, missing your penalty after that, or by missing the people at the grand finale of each game. Some people did not want to suffer the consequences of playing when they tried to use bags for protection, before they were told that they were being wimps. Some people seem willing to torch their self-respect in exchange for less pain. Dear, O dear!

Day 7 Evening

After this it was a chance to let our bodies recover after their thorough workout. So we thought another episode of the Road Mender series was called for, with some Belgian Buns being offered around by Patrick. While, there were also Hot Cross Buns on offer as well. This was before our big plan was going to be put into action tonight.

Day 7 – 8 Night

Tonight was the night that we would complete the challenge after a week of learning about the Centre. We would have to capture the Leader's Headquarters and tape a sheet of paper with our names on it to the wall of their HQ as evidence of its capture. The centre told us about this extra challenge that had never been done before on the day we arrived, but no one appeared to be interested because of the toughness of it; however we were certainly interested. It was clear that it was going to be hard to capture the leader's headquarters cabin. There was a moat around it and one drawbridge that could only be operated from the cabin side. The four of us had to show what we were capable of. Swimming is prohibited, so we thought long and hard all week as to how we could get across. We came up with the idea of using our mattresses and sticks to steer to get across the moat and it worked. Now we had got across the moat, there was a wall. We couldn't climb it because it was too dangerous and the door, in the wall, was locked. Then Jonathan suggested that we build a tunnel. In response I told him that he was getting into the realms of fantasy. We decided to get a ladder out of the maintenance shed. After we used the ladder to climb over the wall, there was just the cabin left to enter. Fortunately, Noah saw that someone had left a window open so we all just hopped through that. We were now in. We taped our sheet of paper to the wall, next to the notice board, and then slipped out of the window. We then realised that the ladder was on the other side of the wall, do were stick on this side of the moat. Thus, we decided to just sleep in the cabin. We woke up off the floor in the morning, leaving no doubt that we weren't pampered or mollycoddled, which gave an inner sense of victory. We popped next door where our sheet of paper was and all four of the leaders were looking at it with their jaws quite low. There was acknowledgement of our capture of their Headquarters.

Day 8 morning Free day in Inverness

On the journey to Inverness from the centre after packing everything up this morning was pretty straight forward after a very eventful week. As today was our last day in the Highlands we were given free time in Inverness for the day before our night-train in the evening. Of course, we went go-karting to implement the new skills that we had learnt.

After this, we were passing by a cinema and Jonathan noticed a film poster about racing. We thought, why not? After a nice, energising cinema experience, we were thinking lunch, so we went to a fast food restaurant for some lovely burgers and fries. Delicious! We still had some free time left so Patrick suggested we visit the cathedral, and we all thought that was a great idea. The spiritual experience was amazing. After leaving the cathedral we made our way to the coach.

Coach to Inverness station Day 8 evening

After we boarded the coach we headed to Inverness Train Station, and soon boarded the sleeper train to London.

Day 8 evening reflection

The trip had been a mixture of preparation for our Geography project but also an opportunity to learn and enjoy different aspects of the Highlands. This was a good idea, I thought, because it meant that the potential of the trip was maximised. The trip wasn't just box ticking but also allowed us to learn about a different culture, to what we were used to back in England.

Night Train Day 8-9

The cabin lodgings on the train had stayed the same, so the four of us were able to relax knowing that we would still be around other people that we could trust. We all gathered in the conference room because I suppose on the train it was the social hub. It was much bigger than our cabins and there were lots of people to talk to. It can be nice to talk to people that you don't usually talk to, as well. When we went back to our cabins after the curfew, it was a rare occasion when I was starting to fall asleep before I had even brushed my teeth. I suppose it had been quite an exhausting week. The four of us in our cabin got to sleep very quickly that night, and before you knew it we were approaching London again after we woke up in the morning. We didn't have to get the tube which saved us from all of that trekking to get down to the train and then back up to street level after getting off the train.

Trip reflection Day 9 morning

From this trip I learned that by not treating certain students like royalty or as if I was honoured that I should be speaking to them or in their presence, when they are a fellow student like everyone else, was liberating. I learned that being inside the circle, and not adhering to the unwritten student hierarchy that had somehow been created, was a good place to be.

Printed in Great Britain
by Amazon